Young Heroes

Ashley Shuyler

Founder of AfricAid

Rachel Lynette

KIDHAVEN PRESS

An imprint of Thomson Gale, a part of The Thomson Corporation

Detroit • New York • San Francisco • New Haven, Conn. • Waterville, Maine • London

For more information, contact:
KidHaven Press
27500 Drake Rd.
Farmington Hills, MI 48331-3535
Or you can visit our Internet site at http://www.gale.com

LIBRARY OF CONGRESS CATALOGING-IN-PUBLICATION DATA

Lynette, Rachel.
Ashley Shuyler : Founder of AfricAid / by Rachel Lynette.
p. cm. — (Young heroes)
Includes bibliographical references and index.
ISBN 978-0-7377-3669-4 (hardcover)
1. Shuyler, Ashley Lauren, 1985– —Juvenile literature. 2. AfricAid, Inc.—Juvenile literature. 3. Young volunteers in social service—United States—Biography—Juvenile literature. 4. Charities—Tanzania—Juvenile literature. 5. Poor—Services for—Tanzania—Juvenile literature. 6. Role models—United States—Biography—Juvenile literature. I. Title.
HV28.S56L95 2007
370.92—dc22
[B]

2007007027

ISBN-10: 0-7377-3669-0

Printed in the United States of America

Contents

Introduction

Making an Impact

When Ashley Shuyler was eleven years old she traveled to Tanzania with her parents. What she experienced there changed her life forever. Ashley was deeply touched by the people she met who lived in **poverty** and yet treated her and her family with extraordinary kindness. She began to realize how lucky she was to live in the United States where she had plenty of clothing, food, and educational opportunities.

Ashley did not forget the people she met in Tanzania. When she was fourteen she started AfricAid. AfricAid is a **nonprofit organization** dedicated to helping children, especially girls, in Africa to get an education. Since its beginnings in 2001, AfricAid has raised hundreds of thousands of dollars to help children in Africa. Among other things, it has funded scholarships, sent school supplies, and built classrooms. Ashley herself has traveled to Africa several times

Much more than learning to read and write, the students at the Maasai Girls' School discover the confidence and bright outlook on the future that can come with an education.

and has even taught at a girls' school in Tanzania. Today, AfricAid continues to grow and to find new ways to make a positive impact in the lives of people who live in Africa.

Chapter One

From Colorado to Tanzania

Ashley Lauren Shuyler was born in New York City on February 26, 1985. She is the only child of parents Richard and Nina Shuyler. Her father works in the airline industry, and her mother worked as a research nurse. When Ashley was just a year old the family moved from New York to Houston, Texas.

A Happy Childhood

Ashley enjoyed her childhood in Houston and has many happy memories of playing with the other children on her street. She was an active child who enjoyed playing outside and climbing trees. She took gymnastics lessons and played on a basketball team for several years. Ashley also loved to read and to do projects with her family and friends. She remembers having a lemonade stand, publishing a neighborhood newspaper, and creating handmade gifts for her teachers, family, and friends.

Ashley has always enjoyed giving to others and says that at least some of the reason for this is because of the school that she attended. "I was really lucky to go to a school that emphasized giving back to the community," says Ashley. Ashley's parents also encouraged her to give to others. Ashley regularly gave a part of her allowance to charities including the World Wildlife Fund and an organization that helps poor children in developing countries. "I think that my family and my teachers have always encouraged me to look beyond myself and use what I've been blessed with to help others,"[1] says Ashley.

As a child, Ashley was not only involved in sports and other activities, she also learned the importance of giving back to the community.

When Ashley was nine years old the family moved again, this time to Golden, Colorado. Ashley was sad to leave her friends in Houston, but she quickly made new friends in Golden. Ashley was used to meeting new people because her family traveled a great deal.

Because Ashley's father worked in the airline industry, he was able to take his family to many places around the world. The family traveled to Europe, Japan, Australia, and New Zealand all before Ashley was

Traveling with her parents, Ashley Shuyler was exposed to many parts of the world at a young age. Here, she and her dad pose by the Coliseum in Rome, Italy, in 1992.

eleven years old. "I was really fortunate to be able to be exposed to other cultures and other ways of life at a young age."[2] says Ashley.

Trip to Tanzania

When Ashley was eleven her family went on a **safari** in Tanzania for three weeks. The family traveled through several different national parks and saw many different kinds of animals. To Ashley the trip was a wonderful adventure. She loved seeing lions, zebras, and other wild animals in their natural habitat. But it was the Tanzanian people, not the animals, that affected Ashley the most.

One of Ashley's most profound experiences happened on the first day while the family was traveling from the airport to their hotel. The driver stopped at an intersection and they rolled down a window to get some fresh air. Immediately, the open window was filled with the hands of children reaching out to them, grabbing them, begging for money, and pleading with them to buy things. Ashley wrote about the experience in an essay:

> In the instant of my shock, I caught sight of a lone pair of eyes amidst the sea of hands. In the split-second that my hazel eyes were locked with those dark, brown eyes, I saw a profound look of emptiness that I had never seen before. I realized that the poverty that afflicted those eyes was worse than the lack of food or clothing that I had seen only moments before. No, those eyes reflected poverty so profound that it leaves a body hollow, with the resulting void destined to be filled by hopelessness.[3]

Touched by Kindness

As they traveled through the country, Ashley saw many people living in poverty. She saw children begging on the side of the road or playing instruments to make some money for their families. Although it was hard for Ashley to see children even younger than she was living in such poor conditions, she was touched by their kindness.

Many times throughout their trip, the local people who were working on the safari went out of their way to be kind to Ashley and her family. For example, on her mother's birthday, a group of them surprised her with a cake that they had managed to cook over an open fire. Ashley and her family were awed by how they had worked so hard to honor her mother on her birthday.

During the trip Ashley's family became especially close to their driver, a man named Rasul. They soon discovered that they had more in common with Rasul than they had at first thought. One day Rasul asked Ashley's father, Richard, if he knew a man named Harlan Shuyler. Richard told Rasul that Harlan was his father and that he had died just a year ago. Rasul began to cry and told the family how he had known Richard's father.

In the early 1990s Richard's father had worked in Tanzania as a part of USAID, a U.S. government agency that helps other countries. Harlan had been teaching people in Tanzania how to protect their crops from insects. Rasul had been his driver. When his time in Tanzania was over, Harlan wrote a letter that helped Rasul to get a job as a safari driver, which is one of the best jobs in Tanzania. Ashley was amazed at the connection between Rasul and her own grandfather.

Ashley marvels at the sight of bathing hippos on her first trip to Tanzania at the age of eleven.

One of Ashley's last memories of Rasul and Tanzania is about what happened when she and her parents were getting on the plane to go home. Rasul came up to Ashley and said to her, "Ashley, please don't forget me when you go home to America."[4] Ashley knew then that she would never forget him or what she had experienced in Tanzania.

On her first trip to Tanzania, Ashley bonded with her safari driver Rasul, pictured. Their friendship made a lasting impression on Ashley.

Returning Home

Ashley realized many things about her life when she was in Tanzania. "The whole time that I spent there, I kept feeling very, very blessed," says Ashley, "and I realized how many incredible opportunities I had back at home and that I could use them to help other people, to help the people that I was meeting while I was there."[5]

Before she and her family left, they had asked the people that they had gotten to know in Tanzania if there was anything they could do for them. One of the most popular requests was to send tennis shoes. Even though the people who worked on the safari had some of the best-paying jobs in the country, it still cost them over a month of wages to buy a pair. Ashley and her family sent several care packages back to Tanzania and stayed in contact with some of the people they had met.

Ready to Help

Ashley told her parents that she wanted to do more to help the people in Tanzania. Her parents understood that she wanted to do something bigger than care packages and encouraged her to take some time to think about what she wanted to do. Ashley took her parents' advice and spent some time thinking about the people in Africa. When she was fourteen, Ashley told her parents that she was ready to take action.

Early Challenges

Once she knew she was ready to do something, Ashley began looking for ways that she could help the people in Tanzania. She remembered how the people she had met had asked for tennis shoes. So, her first idea was to send shipments of clothing. It did not take long for Ashley to run into her first roadblock. She soon discovered that Tanzania had very high **import taxes**. Import taxes are fees that a country's government charges on products that are brought into the country. Tanzania's import taxes were so high that it would cost much too much money to send the clothes there.

Ashley was disappointed but she did not give up. She kept looking for a way to help the people in Tanzania. She did research online and even tried to contact the United Nations. "I was determined to find something that I could do," says Ashley. "Even if I was just a kid, I knew there had to be a way that I could help." [6]

Finding a Path

Ashley found her way to help when a couple came to her church to talk about the Maasai Girls' Lutheran Secondary School, a boarding school in Tanzania that

On her first trip to Tanzania in 1996, Ashley Shuyler felt a strong connection to the people she met. She became determined to help them in any way she could.

they had helped to start. The school was unique because it was the only school in Tanzania to offer a secondary education to Maasai girls.

Ashley learned about the Maasai tribe, which is one of about 120 tribes in Tanzania. She learned that the Maasai are a **nomadic** people who earn their living by raising cattle. Maasai men own and care for the cattle. Maasai women are married off in arranged marriages between the ages of twelve and sixteen, often to men much older than themselves. Maasai men are not limited to just one wife, so often a girl finds that she is just one of several wives. Girls typically become mothers early and are responsible for taking care of the home and the children. Life is often hard for these girls. They live in small mud huts without electricity or running water. Tasks like getting water and collecting firewood can take several hours each day. Maasai customs require them to be quiet and obedient to their husbands, and they can be beaten for failing to do so.

Maasai children do not get much education. Most of the children attend at least some primary school, but only some of the boys go on to secondary school. Traditionally, the Maasai have not seen the value in educating their girls. With only a few years of education, most Maasai girls have no other choice except to become wives and mothers.

Ashley was immediately intrigued with the Maasai people. Although there were things about their culture that she found difficult to accept, she also felt admiration and respect for their way of life. The Maasai are known around the world for their beautifully beaded jewelry

This mud hut is a typical Maasai home. It does not have electricity or running water.

and bright clothing. She realized how pressure from the outside world was changing their way of life. She wanted to help the Maasai people, especially the girls, so that they would have more choices about what they wanted to do with their lives. Listening to the speakers at her church, she began to see how education could give the girls more opportunities. According to Ashley, "It was so amazing when I heard them speaking about the school. I knew immediately that I had found a way in which I could help because my education has always been something that I have valued so much. I just couldn't think of a better thing to do than to help other girls my own age on the other side of the world receive an education."[7]

Ashley talked with the speakers after their presentation. Together they decided that the best thing she could do to help the Maasai school would be to raise money for **scholarships.** The girls needed scholarships to pay the tuition because their families were much too poor to pay it themselves. Each scholarship meant that another girl could be educated.

AfricAid

Ashley told everyone she knew about the Maasai people and school in Tanzania. Many people wanted to help. Two of these people were her neighbors Deborah and Randy Komisarek, one an accountant and the other an attorney. They offered to write the legal docu-

Once AfricAid was founded, fund-raisers were held, such as this silent-auction in 2003, to raise money for scholarships.

ments needed to start a nonprofit organization dedicated to helping girls in Africa get an education.

It took a long time to become a nonprofit organization because the government looks carefully at organizations that send money out of the country. Ashley had a clear vision for what the nonprofit organization should do so she helped to write the mission statement. Ashley also came up with the name "AfricAid." In June 2000 AfricAid, Inc., was incorporated as a nonprofit corporation. In March 2001 AfricAid received its tax-exempt status from the **Internal Revenue Service.** This meant that like other charitable organizations, AfricAid could operate in the United States without paying taxes. AfricAid was born.

Early Successes

Now that AfricAid had been born, it needed to grow. In order to help the girls in Tanzania, Ashley had to let people know about AfricAid and get them to believe in their mission. With the help of her parents and other volunteers, Ashley formed a board of directors, created a brochure, and began holding fund-raisers to raise money for scholarships. She also wrote the content for the AfricAid Web site. Ashley's cousin, Kristen, designed the Web site as a Christmas present. Ashley often tells people that it was one of the best presents she ever received.

In the fall of 2001 AfricAid had its first fund-raiser; a barbecue and **silent auction.** Ashley, who was then sixteen years old, gave a short presentation at the event. During her presentation she talked about how education

Ashley and her mom load a truckful of school supplies for the Maasai Girls' School.

can be a positive solution for "giving people greater opportunities, and for empowering them to make choices in their own lives."[8] Even though it was a small fund-raiser, Ashley was excited that they were finally raising money to help people in Africa.

Another of AfricAid's early successes involved working with another charitable organization to fill an entire cargo container full of school supplies for the Maasai Girls' School. They did this by sponsoring several school supply drives at local churches and schools. In

The first shipment of school supplies is packed up by supporters of AfricAid from the Evergreen Rotary Club.

addition to nineteen computers, the shipment included much-needed supplies such as chalk, pens, solar-powered calculators, and paper. Paper was especially important because although the girls attended classes, they often did not have paper on which to take notes. Because the supplies were shipped directly to the school, they were not subject to Tanzania's import fees.

AfricAid in Action

Ashley continued to work with AfricAid during her teen years, but she also found time to do the other things that she loved. Ashley enjoyed photography and spending time with her friends and family, as well as hiking and biking around Colorado. In addition, she played volleyball, basketball, and lacrosse on her high school teams.

Climbing Kilimanjaro

At the start of 2003, when Ashley was seventeen years old, she and her parents went back to Tanzania. One of the reasons they went was to participate in a fund-raising climb of Mount Kilimanjaro. The climb was hosted by another nonprofit organization, the Evergreen Rotary Club. They were raising money to help fund an African hospital. Ashley and her parents were raising money to pay for more scholarships for the Maasai girls. In this type of fund-raiser, people and organizations sponsor the participants in the form of donations.

The climb took five days. At 19,340 feet (5,894.8m), Kilimanjaro is Africa's highest mountain. A group of ten people hiked about twenty miles over rocky terrain to get to the final camp which was located at 15,000 feet (4,572m). The climb to the summit and back down to the camp had to be done in one day because the air is too thin at the summit for camping. They left camp at midnight to make the final push to the summit. At 9 A.M. on February 7, six of the climbers, including Ashley and her father, made it to the summit. The climb raised $25,000 for AfricAid.

Visiting the Maasai Girls' School

Climbing Mount Kilimanjaro was exciting, but for Ashley, the most thrilling part of the trip to Tanzania was visiting the Maasai Girls' School. After hearing about the school, sending supplies, and raising money for scholarships, Ashley and her family finally got to see where all their hard work was going. The school is not far from Mount Kilimanjaro. It is located on a coffee plantation about 45 miles (72.4k) from the city of Arusha in northeast Tanzania. Since it is a boarding school it has dormitories as well as classrooms. About 250 girls attend the school.

The highlight of the visit was meeting the first ten "AfricAid scholars" who were just starting their educations. The girls were extremely shy. They spoke very little and kept their heads down but were clearly happy to meet Ashley. The girls showed their appreciation for the help that AfricAid was giving them by presenting Ashley with

Ashley Shuyler, pictured on Mt. Kilimanjaro in 2003. She, along with a group of others, scaled Africa's highest mountain in order to raise money for AfricAid.

some traditional Maasai jewelry that they had made just for her.

Ashley also met some of the girls who had been at the school for several years and were soon to graduate. These girls were very different from their younger classmates. They were confident, outspoken, and curious. They asked Ashley many questions about her life in America. Ashley was struck by the difference: "It was amazing to see the difference that four years of education makes for these girls. They start out as shy, young girls who are afraid to raise their voices above a whisper. But by the time they finish school, they are confident, poised, and articulate, ready to make positive changes in their own lives and the lives of those around them."[9]

Ashley meets with students at the Maasai Girls' School in Tanzania. About 250 girls attend the school.

The girls who graduate from the school have many opportunities. Some of the girls continue their educations at colleges that train them to become nurses or teachers. Girls who do exceptionally well can go on to become doctors and lawyers. Some of the girls return to their villages to become wives and mothers. These girls go back to their homes changed and empowered by their educations and work to bring change to their villages. They almost always teach their families and the other people in their community what they have learned. So in many cases, by educating just one girl the school actually educates an entire community. In addition, studies have shown that education plays a huge role in reducing incidences of AIDS and other diseases.

Visiting the school helped Ashley to understand how her work with AfricAid had touched many lives.

Losinoni School

While in Tanzania, Ashley and seven other AfricAid volunteers traveled to the remote village of Losinoni in northern Tanzania. The people there welcomed them warmly. While they were there they visited the village school and learned that it had only a few classrooms to serve over 400 children. They decided that AfricAid would fund the construction of two new classrooms for the village.

AfricAid funded the construction of two new classrooms for the village of Losinoni in northern Tanzania.

A year and a half later Ashley and several other AfricAid volunteers returned to Losinoni to help put the finishing touches on the new classrooms. They sanded, painted, and did whatever else they could to help. They also found time to have fun. The volunteers taught the children in Losinoni how to play the American games of Frisbee and softball. But according to Ashley, "The biggest hit of all was the Polaroid camera that we brought with us to document our stay there. The kids loved seeing themselves instantly on film, and it was wonderful to be able to leave so many pictures there with them." [10]

When the classrooms were finished, the village held a formal dedication ceremony. There were songs, dances, and gifts of traditional Maasai jewelry. The community

Ashley Shuyler, standing center, and several other AfricAid volunteers in Losinoni helping with the final touches on the new classrooms.

A Losinoni villager is surrounded by her jewelry supplies. She and others work to creates pieces of Maasai jewelry that are sold to fund the Losinoni school lunch program.

also presented the volunteers with a goat, something that is highly prized in the Maasai culture. Rather than taking the goat back on the plane to America, they donated it to the school, asking them to sell it to buy school lunches for the children.

Losinoni School Lunch

While they were in Losinoni finishing the classrooms, the village head-woman talked to Ashley about starting a school lunch program for the children of the village. Most of the children in the school ate only one meal of corn porridge in the evening. On empty stomachs, many of the children walked several miles to and from school. The lack of food was endangering the children's

By purchasing these sewing machines for a Tanzanian vocational school, AfricAid is helping young women to learn a skill so they may provide for themselves.

health and making it difficult for them to focus on their schoolwork.

AfricAid suggested a way for the women to start a small business to fund the school lunch program. AfricAid would give the women of the village seed money to buy supplies to make beaded bracelets and key chains. AfricAid would sell the key chains and bracelets in the United States and the proceeds would be used to pay for lunches for the children. The "Maasai Mamas" greeted the idea with enthusiasm and set to work. Soon they had made enough bracelets and key chains for AfricAid to bring back to the United States. AfricAid volunteers sold the bracelets at AfricAid events. Remarkably, when a person buys two bracelets or key chains for $25, it pays for a Losinoni child to have lunch for an entire year!

Other Projects

Since 2001 AfricAid has raised over $350,000. It has funded 170 one-year scholarships. It has built more classrooms and has continued to donate more school supplies and textbooks to schools in Tanzania, Zambia, and Ethiopia. In addition, it has purchased twenty sewing machines for a vocational center that helps very poor girls in Tanzania to learn a trade so that they do not have to live on the streets.

Chapter Four

A Life of Service

Although Ashley loves the time she has spent in Tanzania, most of her work for AfricAid takes place in the United States. Ashley does many things to raise awareness about what she has seen and learned in Africa and to raise money to fund AfricAid's projects. She does a great deal of writing for AfricAid, including much of the information on the AfricAid Web site and its semi-annual newsletter. She has given numerous presentations at schools and churches and to other organizations. She has also been interviewed on television and on the radio and has been featured in Internet and newspaper articles about AfricAid.

Honors for Ashley

In addition, Ashley has been recognized for her work by several organizations. In 2001 Ashley received the Gloria Barron Young Heroes Prize. She donated the $2,000 prize money to AfricAid to fund Maasai scholarships. In 2002 she was selected as a winner at the Celebration for Young

Entrepreneurs, an event sponsored by the Young Americans Center for Financial Education. In 2003 Ashley received the National Prudential Spirit of Community award. This award also came with a cash prize which she donated to AfricAid. In 2007 Ashley was selected as a finalist for the Do Something BRICK award. These awards are given to young people who create positive social change.

Ashley also continued to make her own education a top priority. She graduated high school with honors in June 2003 and was accepted at Harvard University in Massachusetts. She decided to continue to learn about

While most of the work that Ashley Shuyler does for AfricAid is done from the United States, she cherishes the time that she gets to spend in Africa on her visits.

Africa and other countries by majoring in social studies with a focus on underdeveloped countries.

Teaching in Tanzania

When Ashley was twenty years old she took some time off from school to teach at the Maasai Girls' School. Ashley went with her college roommate, Liz Panarelli. Both Ashley and Liz received grants for international **internships** from Harvard, which funded their trips. Ashley and Liz lived on campus at the school for four months.

In 2005 Ashley and her college roommate Liz Panarelli, left, spent four months teaching new students at the Maasai Girls' School.

Ashley and Liz gather a group of students for a game of "duck, duck, goose," which they renamed to "stay, stay, run," in order to help the students practice their English.

They taught English, math, geography, and sports and games (PE) to the incoming students. The classes they taught were part of a special program that the girls go through before they start their first year of school. Because the girls come from many different places and are at different levels in their education, this four-month program helps to get them all to the same place before the start of the school year.

One of the main purposes of the program was to get the girls up to speed in their English. In Tanzania children are taught in their native language of **Swahili** in primary school. Although they are also taught English, often they do not learn the language very well. This can be challenging because secondary school is taught in English, not Swahili. Fortunately, Ashley had taken Swahili in school, so she could communicate with the girls who were still struggling to learn the English language.

Ashley and Liz did much more than teach at the Maasai school. They also helped the girls to make the transition from living in a rural village with their families to living at a boarding school. During this time Ashley learned even more about the Maasai people and developed an even deeper love and respect for them. Ashley describes the experience as being "the most amazing four months of my life" and says that she may have learned more from the students than they learned from her. "These young girls are just wonderfully amazing people. As I got to know them and learn their stories, I continued to feel humbled by their strength, their determination, their resiliency,"[11] says Ashley.

Committed to Their Studies

Ashley was extremely impressed by how seriously the girls took their education and how much it meant to them. One girl told Ashley that she had walked ten miles to and from her primary school each day. Most of the girls were giving up arranged marriages in their villages to attend school. Many of the girls faced disapproval from their villages and some of the girls had been completely rejected by their families because of their choice to get an education. These girls could never return home again.

However, this was not the case for all of the girls. Ashley returned home with one of the students, a girl named Uzuri. Ashley was fascinated by how Uzuri was able to step outside the bounds of the Maasai customs about how a girl should behave. "Due to her education, her role is much more one of her own creation than the roles of those around her,"[12] observed Ashley. Uzuri did many things that her sisters were too afraid to do, like drinking tea in front of the men and talking with her father after dinner. Many of the people in the village treated her with more respect than they did the other girls of the village. One woman even told Uzuri that she would like her own children to attend school as well.

In the Maasai culture, the education of females is generally met with disapproval. The students at the Maasai Girls' School, however, are determined to continue with their studies despite what their families might think.

While Ashley was at the school the first group of AfricAid scholars graduated. This was an exciting event for Ashley as well as for the seven graduates. The girls wore traditional Maasai beaded gowns for their special day. Over the past four years they had devoted themselves to their studies. But the experience of being at the school had given them much more than an education. Unlike most other Maasai girls, these girls were confident, outgoing, and excited about their futures. "They were so happy and proud,"[13] says Ashley.

Future of AfricAid

Ashley plans to continue to stay involved in AfricAid. She is excited about how the organization is growing

Ashley was honored to see the first group of AfricAid scholars graduate from the Maasai Girls' School in 2005.

AfricAid began because Ashley Shuyler had a wish to help others. Today, it continues to grow and to find new ways to make a positive impact in the lives of people who live in Africa.

and about the projects it will do in the future. "It's really exciting because, as AfricAid continues to grow and expand, its reach in Tanzania has grown in ways we never would have imagined possible when we were first getting started,"[14] says Ashley.

AfricAid is committed to continuing to fund scholarships, provide school supplies, and build classrooms, but it also plans to improve the quality of education in Africa. One of AfricAid's future goals is to become more involved in training teachers. AfricAid has plans to help provide teacher training programs for African teachers so they can learn teaching methods that encourage more participation, leadership, and critical thinking skills. These are the skills that the students need in order to change their own futures, as well as those of their communities and even of their countries.

What You Can Do

Even though Ashley is no longer a child herself, she believes that children have a great deal of power and that they should not see their age as a disadvantage. "It's been my experience that adults are very excited and inspired by kids who want to make a difference in their own communities and in the world,"[15] says Ashley. She recommends that kids who are passionate about making a positive change should tell everyone they know about what they want to do. If she had not told her neighbors about her dream of helping girls at the Maasai school, AfricAid might never have been created.

Ashley also suggests that children consider their own gifts and talents and use those to help others. For example, if you can sing or play a musical instrument, you could put on a concert and donate the proceeds from the ticket sales to your cause. If you like to bake, you could have a bake sale to raise money. If you enjoy making crafts you could sell them. The AfricAid Web site has many ideas for kids who want to help.

Children are an important part of the AfricAid fundraising team. Children all over the United States have formed AfricAid clubs to help raise money for AfricAid projects. In addition, kids can collect school supplies for AfricAid to send to Tanzania. Children can also help to raise awareness by talking to the people they know about the challenges that children in Africa face. AfricAid welcomes help from young people and their Web site is full of ideas about how to get involved.

Notes

Chapter One: From Colorado to Tanzania

1. Ashley Shuyler, interview with author, November 17, 2006.
2. Shuyler, interview.
3. Ashley Shuyler, "Founder's Messages: Why Was AfricAid Founded?" AfricAid. www.africaid.com/messages/index.shtml.
4. Shuyler, interview.
5. Shuyler, interview.

Chapter Two: Ready to Help

6. Shuyler, interview.
7. Shuyler, interview.
8. Shuyler, interview.

Chapter Three: AfricAid in Action

9. Shuyler, interview.
10. Ashley Shuyler, "Recent Projects: Losinoni," AfricAid. www.africaid.com/recent/index.shtml.

Chapter Four: A Life of Service

11. Shuyler, interview.
12. Ashley Shuyler, "The Global Ties That Bind: From One Classroom to Another," *AfricAid Newsletter,* September 2006.
13. Shuyler, interview.
14. Shuyler, interview.
15. Shuyler, interview.

Glossary

import taxes: Fees that the government charges on goods that are brought into the country.

Internal Revenue Service: The branch of the U.S. Treasury Department that is responsible for collecting taxes.

internships: Programs that allow students to get training for a profession in the field.

nomadic: Not having a permanent home, but moving from place to place with the seasons.

nonprofit organization: An organization that operates not to make a profit but rather to support a cause such as a school or charity.

poverty: The state of being extremely poor.

safari: A trip across a stretch of land in Africa for the purpose of hunting or observing wild animals.

scholarships: An amount of money granted to promising students to help fund their education.

silent auction: An event where goods or services are sold to people who bid on them by writing their bids down.

Swahili: The official language of Tanzania.

For Further Exploration

Books

Sondra Clark, *You Can Change the World! Creative Ways to Volunteer & Make a Difference.* Grand Rapids, MI: Revell, 2003. This book, written by a thirteen-year-old, offers 150 ways for kids to make the world a better place.

Rennay Craats, *Indigenous People: Maasai.* New York: Weigl, 2005. This book offers a wealth of information on the history, lifestyle, and traditions of the Maasai people. Includes color pictures, glossary, and bibliography.

Harvey Croze, *Africa for Kids: Exploring a Vibrant Continent.* Chicago: Chicago Review, 2006. This informative book covers information about Africa and also includes nineteen craft and cooking activities.

Barbara A. Lewis, *The Kid's Guide to Social Action: How to Solve the Social Problems You Choose—and Turn Creative Thinking into Positive Action.* Minneapolis, MN: Free Spirit, 1998. This book gives step-by-step instructions on ways to get involved in social action. Also includes stories of kids and teens who made a difference.

Chin Oi Ling, *Welcome to Tanzania*. Milwaukee, WI: Gareth Stevens, 2005. This informative book offers information about Tanzania. Includes full-color photographs.

Web Sites

AfricAid (www.africaid.com). AfricAid's official Web site, created by Ashley Shuyler and her cousin Kristen, offering a wealth of information about Ashley, AfricAid, and how to help.

DO Something (www.dosomething.org). This Web site encourages young people to make positive changes in the world. It includes information on how to get involved and on what other young people are doing. Home of the BRICK awards.

Maasai (http://laleyio.com). This site offers information about the history and culture of the Maasai people, including many pictures and samples of their music.

Index

Picture Credits

Cover: Liz Panarelli. Courtesy of Ashley Shuyler

Courtesy of Ashley Shuyler, 5, 17, 18, 21, 30, 34, 37

Photo by Danny Dodson. Courtesy of Ashley Shuyler, 37

Photo by Liz Panarelli. Courtesy of Ashley Shuyler, 39

Photo by Nina Shuyler. Courtesy of Ashley Shuyler, 7, 8, 11, 12, 15, 26, 28, 33, 35

Photo by Rick Shuyler. Courtesy of Ashley Shuyler, 25, 29, 38

Photo by Carolyn Taylor. Courtesy of Ashley Shuyler, 20

About the Author

Rachel Lynette has written over a dozen other books for children as well as many articles on children and family life. She also teaches science to children of all ages. Rachel lives in the Seattle area in the Songaia Cohousing Community with her two children, David and Lucy, a cat named Cosette, and two playful rats. When she is not teaching or writing she enjoys spending time with her family and friends, traveling, reading, drawing, inline skating, crocheting hats, and eating chocolate ice cream.